guillotine

Also by Eduardo C. Corral

Slow Lightning

guillotine

poems

EDUARDO C. CORRAL

Graywolf Press

This publication is made possible, in part, by the voters of Minnesota through a Minnesota State Arts Board Operating Support grant, thanks to a legislative appropriation from the arts and cultural heritage fund. Significant support has also been provided by Target, the McKnight Foundation, the Lannan Foundation, the Amazon Literary Partnership, and other generous contributions from foundations, corporations, and individuals. To these organizations and individuals we offer our heartfelt thanks.

Published by Graywolf Press
250 Third Avenue North, Suite 600
Minneapolis, Minnesota 55401

www.graywolfpress.org

Published in the United States of America

ISBN 978-1-64445-030-7

2 4 6 8 9 7 5 3

Library of Congress Control Number: 2019949953

Cover design: Carlos Esparza

Cover art: *I have eyes where they can best protect me*, 2019. Ink, acrylic, embroidery, twine, cut paper, and egg tempura on canvas. © Felipe Baeza. Courtesy Maureen Paley, London.

for the caretakers

Contents

guillotine

Se juntan aguas   *En el cuerpo*

MYRIAM MOSCONA

Ceremonial

Delirious,
touch-starved,
    I pinch a mole
        on my skin, pull it
off, like a bead—
    I pinch & pull until
        I am holding
a black rosary. Prayer
    will not cool
        my fever.
Prayer will not
    melt my belly fat,
        will not thin
my thighs.

A copper-
faced man once
    called me beautiful.
        Stupid,
stupid man.
    I am obese. I am
        worthless.
I can still feel
    his thumb—
        warm,
burled—moving
    in my mouth.
        His thumbnail
a flake

of sugar
he would not
    allow me to swallow.
        Desperate
for the sting of snow

on my skin,
            rosary
tight in my fist,
        I walk into
                a closet, crawl
into a wedding dress.
            Oh Lord,
here I am.

Testaments Scratched into a Water Station Barrel

Apá, dying is boring. To pass las horas,
                              I carve
                    our last name
                              all over my body.
I try to recall the taste of Pablo's sweat.
                                        Whiskey, no.
                    Wet dirt, sí.
                              I stuff English
          into my mouth, spit out chingaderas.
                                        Have it your way.
                    Home of the Whopper.
                    Run
for the border. ¡Aguas! The mirror
                              betrayed us.
                    It erased your face
                              from my face.
Gave me mother's smile, narrow nariz.
                                        Once, I wore
                    her necklace.
                    The gold slick,
obscene. God, I was beautiful.
                                        Cada noche,
          I sleep
                    with dead men.
     The coyote was the third to die.
                                        Your money
                    is still in his wallet.
                    Quien engaña
no gana. Apá, there's a foto, in my bolsillo,
                              of a skeleton
                    shrouded
                              in black flames:
     Nuestra Señora de la Santa Muerte.
                                        Patron saint
                    of smugglers, pick-
                              pockets & jotos.
La Flaca. Señora Negra. La Huesuda.

¡Aguas!
An animal
is prowling
this station. It shimmies with hunger.
It shimmers
with thirst.
To keep it away,
I hurl my memories at it. Your laughter is now
snagged
on its fangs.
Your pain
now breathes inside its lungs. Taste
the feeling.
Siempre Coca-Cola.
America's
real choice—I gathered & smashed bottles.
Apá, follow
the glass
snaking from
the barrel to a mesquite to find my body.
Lips blue,
skin thick
with scabs.
Apá, kneel in the shade, peel
the scabs. Touch
our last name.
Solís.

Bought my luck.
Rabbit's foot.
Hiked through paloverde.
Thick heat.
Bullet holes in cacti.
Rested by a ditch.
Sand littered with used tampons.
Took off my sneakers.
Ants crisscrossed my feet.
Sandal straps.
Passed around crackers.
Tuna cans.
Mustard & ketchup packets.
Trekked over three hills.
Dashed across a dirt road.
Nearly stepped on a diamondback.
Quiet coil.
Squatted under mesquite.
Drank hot water.
Tried to forget the plazas of Hermosillo.
Rose bushes.
Roasted cashews.
Tried to remember my uncle's phone number.
A butcher in Iowa.
Ames.
Walked toward a mountain.
Coolness fell through the heat.
Guillotine.
Rested.
Fought off the oldest smuggler.
Yellow teeth.
Gums pink as horse cock.
Woke with some Portuguese in my head.
A morte nós absorvemos inteiramente.
Icy dawn.
Lanced my blisters.
Put on three pairs of socks.

Walked for six hours.
Dunes.
Orange wildflowers.
Twisted my right ankle.
Leaned against a boulder
Too long.
Left behind.
Took off my jacket.
Sweated through my clothes.
Puked tuna.
Remembered my honeymoon.
The coast of Veracruz.
Cheap hotel.
Turned over Jesús before undressing.
Holy velvet.
Puked again.
Took off my shoes.
Wrapped belt around my ankle.
Lurched forward.
Gossiped with the heat.
Laughed.
Found this water station.
Waiting.

wall

rio de **aguas** vivas

is the **soul** a WITNESS

a *huevo* build the fucking wall

voice

rio de **aguas** vivas

is the **soul** a WITNESS make Arizona great

swallowing my   voice   again

swallowing negra

paloma negra

BUILD THE WALL STOP DRUGS

chinga tu madre gringo ™

BUILD   THE WALL STOP DRUGS hey illegals ICE

is coming

bidi

I ♥ brown A$$

rain falling in my throat

rain falling   **bidi bidi** bom bom

tu *Trump*

god

is god touching me // ay México

bom

ven por tu gente die wetbacks

die

In a room with a terracotta doorknob   I slept
for thirty years beneath antlers   beneath
a horsehair blanket   here the hours are so cold
I rub my hands over a still-warm body   god
is nothing more   than a gecko resting on a lemon
nothing more than grass   veiled with dust
please please   lift the veil   all that green
yearning for a kiss   I regret training my mind
like an animal it never bared   its fangs
it never   instinctively leapt to tenderness
there's a harmonica   tattooed on my collarbone
I can feel death's mouth on it   lips wiry & hot

((

la bestia me está
                    siguiendo
el desierto desnuda
        al hueso
como santos
        cago diablos
la muerte
        es un tren
las estrellas
son pasajeros
        yo no yo no
México es lindo
        pero sufrí
tanto

                        sólo borracho
                o dormido
                        se me olvida
                el tren
        de la muerte
                puedo oírlo
        tambores
                de sangre
        veneno gritando
                el desierto
me está comiendo
        soy de un país
                donde el sol
        se levanta
Yoro

                                    In the desert, the moon
        shivers. Tonight, to stay awake, I'll cut my feet
with glass.

                        Outside Oaxaca, in a clinic, my mother said,
"I hate your Indian face."

        In the dream I'm running. My limbs skeletal
& scabbed.

                        After my mother's death, I found, in a box,
her wedding dress.

        As I lifted the lid, a stench corkscrewed
into my nostrils:

                        the lace had curdled like milk. During the day
I gather tinder.

        Paper. Shed snakeskin. When the last light
above the mountains

                        knots into stars, I crouch under mesquite,

                                            make a fire.

        Sometimes the moon stops shivering. Sometimes
I tally what I owe.

                        In the dream I'm running through a hallway.
The floor uneven.

        The walls green. Last month, as my son blew out
the candles

                        on his cake, I noticed, for the first time,
the hideous shape

        of his nose. Tonight I'll pinch my thighs to stay
awake. My mother,

                        in the clinic, said, "The rain has a fever, it
needs plenty

        of rest, it needs to drink plenty of water." The doctor
scribbled in a file

                        then asked for more money. If my mother
could see me now!

        My feet bloody. My face darker than ever.
Tonight, to stay awake,

                        I'll sit close to the fire. In the dream I stumble,

but I never let go
      of my right breast: an urn heavy with my own
ashes, an urn
            I'm lugging God-knows-where.

if you see
a Mexican

walking down
the road &

hit him
just right

you can grease
your truck

                                        Perro que no anda,
                               no encuentra hueso—
                                   through summer, I
        hurry. Blood soaks my sneakers. The handkerchief
                around my head
                        reeks like sobacos.
                If I don't cut into cacti,
        if I don't chew the pulp to draw water out,
my shadow will
        wander away.
Afternoons,
        with nail polish remover, I clean the sores on my feet.
                                        On the bottle,
                                in red print,
                                        a proverb: beauty
        can't be talked into speech. The sky isn't blue.
                It's azul. Saguaros
                        are triste, not curious.
                In México, bodies
        disappear. Bodies, in the Sonoran desert,
are everywhere.
        A headless corpse
sporting a T-shirt
        that reads: Superstar.
                                        A severed hand,
                                black yarn around
                                        the thumb. Welcome
        to the cagada. If I don't look for water under rocks,
                my shadow
                        will wander away—
                another wetback
        veering too close to highways, too close to ranchos.
Coral alighting
        on gold, yellow
alighting on rose.

Dusk, here, is stunning. Yesterday, I woke to ants crawling
over my body,
to ants crawling
over
the body on the cross around my neck.

déjame vivir Señora de las Sombras

Señora de las Sombras salt my tongue

Señora de las Sombras te lo pido por favor

your face your face Señora de las Sombras

Señora de las Sombras devour me

mi mas bello error Señora de las Sombras

Señora de las Sombras he venido a perdirte perdón

your hands your hands Señora de las Sombras

undress my hunger Señora de las Sombras

Señora de las Sombras undress my thirst

Señora de las Sombras spit me out

tu a mi no me hundes Señora de las Sombras

Señora de las Sombras no hay ni dinero ni trabajo

the dead gather Señora de las Sombras

Señora de las Sombras de mi enamorate

que será será Señora de las Sombras

my wounds belong to you Señora de las Sombras

Sometimes a wolf leaps out of a lion   last winter
I almost eloped with my second cousin   plastic
barrettes   in the shape of the Eiffel Tower
keep her bangs from her eyes   newer footpaths
are rigged with sensors   which track
& identify   the first time I saw flowering
ironwood I remembered   the inside of oyster shells
lilac shuddering through ivory   deep in
my guts   there's a delicacy   dozens of condoms
crammed with cocaine   Mexican caviar
on the flatbed of a pickup I greased   my throat
with cooking oil   then swallowed

[[[[

Water too held me hostage   at ten
catching   fireflies with my brothers
the oldest a spectacle   the youngest
a spectator   I fell headfirst into a river
there's a gun tucked   in my left boot
twelve bullets   cackle inside a tin box
three years ago in a bedroom   in Phoenix
I was held for six days   soiled clothes
& spoiled food   heaped in each corner
a television in another room   yelled
in perfect English   shots reported at a school
run hide   secure yourself immediately

𝍤

Dust devil, tattered sail.
        Stray tenderness
stay.

there's a sermon
inside my testicles
everything

is plural in my throat
Costa Rica

is the oldest
the one who wears
a crucifix

once a day
he sheds his shirt
to air

his armpits

the crucifix glints
one by one

we kneel in front of him
forgive us our debts

El Salvador
says the moon
is an upside down

turtle shell
the Mayan symbol
for zero

sweat makes México
horny as hell

twice a week
his mother-in-law

licked salt
off his chest

when we stop listening
does music
alight on branches

does God walk back
into the room

we're down
to one can of Spam

Guatemala

says death is tiptoeing
across our bodies

to marry
our shadows

we're tired
but our cellphones
are charged

hola America hola

                    Sister, we crouched
                behind boulders, dove
        into bushes
                to avoid
        patrol jeeps. Sister,
we drank ditch-
water, caught   of your favorite skirt.
        a rabbit. Sister,   Sister, the long ears
                if he didn't enter   & yellow teeth
        your room,   of the rabbit
                he entered mine.   reminded me
                        I'd stare at glow-   of the piano
                in-the-dark   decaying
            constellations.   in our yard. Ivory
        His mouth   keys, felt hammers.
                carnivorous Sister, to avoid smugglers,
        & slow. Sister,   we crawled
I'll be hiding out   through thorns,
in Raleigh,   scrambled over
        a few blocks   barbed wire. Sister,
            from our cousins,   as he skinned
in a trailer   the rabbit,
            the color   he dropped

            the switchblade. I grabbed it,
    slashed his throat. Sister, his blood sprayed
            into the air. Each drop pitch-
    black & slick. Each drop
            an effigy
    of God.

If you think I look good naked   wait until you see me dead

Before fleeing Toluca   I left a glass of water
in front of a tarnished mirror   my favorite pietà
I didn't beg for pity I   didn't beg for refuge
at night   a graffitied boulder flickers
like a neon jukebox   between the mountains
a crescent moon gleams   like a bus station
urinal   by this light I furiously scratch
I lost my virginity in a shed   it fucking hurt
twice   I spit in my father's face
in my hands   dark blood blood bark
a small ball of scabs   peeled from my flesh
my contraband   my pomegranate

ЖII

clavo
clavo
clavo
clavo
me falta un clavo para mi cruz
clavo
clavo
clavo
clavo
clavo
clavo
clavo
clavo

Far from highways I flicker
        gold the whispering
                    gasoline
if I pinch her nipples
        too hard
                no joy for her
no joy for me
        so I practice on ticks
                    press them
just so so they give
        but do not burst
                    beneath
my boots
        thistle & puncture vine
                a wild horse
asleep on all fours
        its shadow still grazing
                    my lips
black meat
        my tongue
                black meat
in my backpack
        sardine tins
                    saltines
& a few cough drops
        the moon is my library
                    there's a glacier
inside a grain of salt
        do you understand
                I'm sorry
my Albanian
        isn't very good
                    tremble
if God forgets you
        tremble
                if God
remembers you

out of clay I shape
        sparrows
I glaze their bills & claws
    I give them names
        like gossamer
inglenook lagoon
    she bathed
        a trumpet
in milk
    her tenderness acoustic
        & plural
her pupils perched
    in all that green
        there's nudity
around the corner
    bones cracked
        & iridescent
sometimes it rains so hard
    even the moon
        puts on
a raincoat
    zinc razz zinc jazz
        I notch my arms
I notch my thighs
    five six days
        I score
my skin but not
    the back of my knees
        two ovals
two portraits
    my son at ten
        his eyes ablaze
my son at one
    his eyes shut
        once
I dressed him in burlap
    once bicycles

              & marbles
once I tore rain
       out of a parable
              to strike down
his thirst

God is circling like a vulture

gracias nada mas

corazón de oro

a quién vas engañar

I notch letters into mesquite

carta abierta

between insight & proof

la tumba falsa

ay que líos

I said a hurtful thing to my hermano

al sur del bravo

somos mas americanos

an obsidian thorn pierces the moon's ear

deja de llorar chiquilla

I'm counting my sins

te odio y te quiero

tu con el yo con ella

cacti needles pinprick skin

a kind of rain

lo tomas o lo tiras

I drop my rosary

it scurries away like a scorpion

reina de reinas reina del sur

mira mira mira

el avión de la muerte

viva mi Sinaloa

vivan los mojados

Lo que no duele ha dolido.

LUIS MUÑOZ

Guillotine

The scorpions always arrive
      at dawn. Gently,
            their pincers
  touch the cuts
      on my lips. I clutch
          the edges
of the mattress, stare
      at the mirrored ceiling.
          My mouth opens,
  but no sound staggers out.
      The scorpions—
          dark green, dank—
reach in, pull out
    the razor blade
        under my tongue . . .

Two scorpions.
    A razor blade.
        Slowly, in unison,
  without letting go of the metal,
      they move.
          A little guillotine
making its way
    down my body.
      I remember
dragging my thumb
    through his beard,
          coppery & difficult.
The scorpions
    pause, tilt
      the blade.
  A threat, a reminder.
      It's my task to stop yearning
        for as long

as it takes them
        to carry a blade
                across my skin.
    My thoughts swerve
                from monsoon storms
                        to accordions
to pecan groves.
        The little guillotine
                starts moving again.
    I begin to sense
                the enormity of my body.
                        The blade
high in the air.
        For now.

Sentence

I crawl back   he unpacks his tools
oils the wooden handles   rinses the metal

fragrant   his thighs fragrant his sneer

koi & eternity inked on his skin   an ecstatic
blue a bewildered green

some wounds are ovals some wounds are opals
the ears of a white wolf pivot   toward the moon

I flee now & then   alone in the desert for months
a nomad in a kimono of pressed-together dust

beautiful his throat his words   even more beautiful
"it's my turn to ask for a bit more from you"

he likes it when I bleed   strangers once

gently he hammers gold into a sentence   gently
the sentence enters me

after Don McKay

Saguaro

Scrawl of graffiti,
illegible jade,

skin wax-rich,
pleat-rich,

monsoon accordion,
long-legged

hitchhiker thumbing
by the interstate,

summer relic,
wind-broken, wind-

borne, Sonoran
pictograph ablaze

in cloud shadow,
glass lightning, glass

tuning fork,
green forged

into a sword, saber
or claymore,

rainwater pitcher,
ribs porous &

coral, rock-bound
welt, barbed rebozo.

Autobiography of My Hungers

His beard: an avalanche of honey,
    an avalanche
of thorns. In a bar too close to the Pacific,
             he said, "I don't love you,
    but not because I
couldn't be attracted to you." Liar—
           even my soul
is potbellied. Thinness,
    in my mind, equals the gay men
              on the nightly news.
    Kissed by death & public scorn.
The anchorman declaring,
         "Weight loss is one
of the first symptoms." The Portuguese
have a word for imaginary, never-
        to-be-experienced love.
              Whoop-de-doo.
    "I don't love you," he said.
The words flung him back—
         in his eyes, I saw it—
    to another bar
where a woman sidestepped his desire.
        Another hunger.
             Our friendship.
In tenth grade, weeks after
        my first kiss, my mother
said, "You're looking thinner."
    That evening, I smuggled a cake
          into my room.
I ate it with my hands,
    licked buttercream off
        my thumbs until I puked.
    Desire with no future,
bitter longing—

I starve myself by yearning
for intimacy that doesn't
                            & won't exist.
Holding hands on a ferry. Tracing,
                with the tip of my tongue,
a jawline. In a bar too close
                      to the Pacific, he said,
"I don't love you, but not
          because I couldn't be attracted to you."
                           His beard:
an avalanche of thorns,
                an avalanche of honey.

Córdoba

In a bathroom
with turquoise walls,

my reflection bleeds. I reach
to clean, with my thumb,

an oval mirror speckled
with toothpaste

& smeared, now,
with penicillin-rich blood,

then I remember—
pull back my left hand.

I don't touch mirrors. It's wrong,
my father always said,

to touch a man.

Questions for My Body

Why are you nocturnal

How many cathedrals have you entered

Has cruelty ever saved you

Do you remember the length of his thumbs

Isn't that enough cake

Have you ever soaked your feet in gasoline

Do you still fear the virus

How can you sleep in this heat

Is that a soul patch

Did you laugh or cry at Keats's grave

Have you been claimed

Border Patrol Agent

Summer is a puta. I park
                    beneath branches, crank up the AC
                                        in the jeep.
I hate the rearview mirror.
            It makes me look like my father. Chaste
                                & singed. Last week,
beneath a sky Walmart blue,
                in a clearing full of bottles, sneakers,
                                            TP rolls,
I found a body. Legs
                gnawed to the knees, barbed wire tight
                                            around
the throat.
            I remembered graffiti
                        on a boulder: *God*
is always hungry.
            Sometimes, with binoculars,
                                    I watch wild horses
hurry through the heat. Once
                a yearling stopped mid-gallop

then collapsed
            into a bed of coals the rain could not extinguish.
                                        The radio
is always crackling:
            six wets sighted on infrared,
                        need a spic speaker stat . . .
I only speak Spanish with my father.
                    He often mistakes blue parakeets
                                                perched
on the stove for gas flames.
                        Last July, far from Tucson,
                                    I found a rape tree:
torn panties draped on branches.

The tree a warning,
                    a way for smugglers
to claim terrain.
          Lightning climbs a hillside like a stilt walker.
                                        Rain
strikes the windshield.
          I think of my wife
                    asleep on her side. Breasts
pressed together
          as if one were dreaming the other.
                                        Her womb
empty.
          My dick useless.
                    There are things I just can't tell her.
Sometimes only body parts remain.
                    They're buried
in baby caskets.

Song of the Open Road

*US Customs & Border Protection officers can stop a car
within one hundred miles of a border for the following reasons.*

Whether the [body] is close to the border;
whether the [body] is on a known smuggling route;

whether the [body] could have been trying to avoid a checkpoint;
whether the [body] looks unusual in some way;

whether the [body] is of a sort often favored by smugglers;
whether the [body] appears to have been altered or modified;

whether the [body] is being driven in an erratic or unsafe manner;
whether the [body] appears to be traveling in tandem with another [body];

whether the [body] looks as if it has recently been driven off road;
whether the persons in the [body] are paying undue attention to the agent;

whether the persons in the [body] tried to avoid being seen by the agent;
whether the [body] slowed down after seeing the agent.

Lines Written at Federico García Lorca Park

In the cage of my thumbprint I keep my third wish

acoustic winter

Rain undresses music rain undresses his voice

arrow & minaret

Beneath my palm the wiry fur of lust

open body open

A wound is a self-reporting instrument

silver filigree

I sleep with his face under my tongue

scab on water

Black Water

I spit his name out & four wolves
                    appear. Black, eyes
                              silvery, ears skinned
                    & tense.
They thrash their tails twice then
                    rush toward me.
                              A dark pouring.
                    I stagger back,
raise my arms . . .

                              I'd watch him
                                        lather his beard.
                              Once a week,
for a year. An oval mirror
                    held him
                              & doubled
                    his gestures.
His hands quick, odic. The wolves
                    now closer. Close.
                              Their stench arrives
                    first. Decaying
meat, feces. An eye-watering stink
                    that severs me
                              from hunger.
                    The wolves
crash into me. Furious paws, teeth
                    hot & notched,
                              manes teeming
                    with dirt.
Briefly, I'm fording black water.
                    Briefly, I forget
                              his face. Then
                    they vanish.
I spin around. Nothing
                    but sand & sky

                              the color of clay.
                    Even the stench
is gone. I tremble & tremble.
                    Raw my limbs.
                         Then I hear
                    the mirror,
in a room miles away.

                    Furred with frost
                         & lust,
                    it howls.

To Francisco X. Alarcón

(1954–2016)

You made tomatoes laugh
& warned me
some words die in cages.

I met you first in the desert.

You burned sage, greeted
each of the four directions
with plumed syllables.

The ritual embarrassed me—
your stout body, your
mischievous smile did not.

You were familial.

The first poem I wrote
that sounded like me
echoed your work.

Copal, popote, tocayo, cacahuate:
you taught me Spanish
is a colonial tongue.

Some Mesoamerican elders
believed there's a fifth direction.

Not the sky or the ground
but the person right next to you.

I'm turning to face you, maestro.
I'm greeting you.
Tahui.

"Around Every Circle Another Can Be Drawn"

I

In tenth grade, I kissed a guy who called me a faggot once or twice a week.
                                                     I still see his voice:
six hummingbirds nailed to a wall.
                    In an olive grove, outside of Fuente Grande, in 1936,
a teacher, two bullfighters &
        Federico García Lorca were shot to death by fascist soldiers.
                                                     During the Reagan years,
I sweated out new language.
            Kaposi sarcoma. Febrile. Oral candidiasis.
                    Last summer, in Sevilla, I flirted with a stranger.
He pinched my belly, walked away, laughing.
                                Later, along Calle Arjona,
a remix of "Girls Just Want to Have Fun" poured out of a passing taxicab.
                                "Shut the fuck up, Cyndi Lauper!"
I yelled. Mala copa. Joder.
            The soldier who shot Lorca bragged he fired two bullets into his ass
for being queer.
        For years, I desired a man who didn't desire me.
                                He was gentle with my lust.
(I never thanked him. I'm thanking him now.)
                        But once, in a splinter-rich booth, he held my hand.
A kindness I can't forgive.

II

Diminished but quick
      I sprint into the desert
            toward
a dust devil
      slowly twisting
            along a canal
I step
      into the grit
            & whirl
not dust
      after all
            but a spiral
of locusts
      each a coil of gold
            oiled
with honey
      long hind legs
            click click
click
      not one skims
            my skin
a thunderhead
      on the horizon
            shimmers
half-built
      cathedral
            what a saint said
about God
      I believe about
            loneliness
a circle
      whose center is
            everywhere
& its circumference
      nowhere

Commercial Break

Another corpse—sunburnt face, broken legs.

Recovered a few miles from Ajo, in a cholla thicket.

One personal belonging found with corpse.

A red Nike sneaker.

To a Straight Man

All zodiac all
        radar your voice
                I carried it
across the Atlantic
        to Barcelona
                I photographed
cathedrals
        cacti mosaic
                salamanders
I even photo-
        graphed my lust
                always
your voice skimming
        her skin
                mattress springs
so noisy so birdlike
        you filled her room
                with cages
camera bright
        in my pocket
                map
unfolding
        in my mind
                I explored a park
leaves notched
        & enormous
                graffitied boulders
then
        three men
                tall & clean
closed in
        they broke open
                my body
with their fists
        insufferable

　　　　　　　　　your red wool cap
insufferable the way
　　　　　you walked
　　　　　　　　　away from me
come back please
　　　　　the buttons
　　　　　　　　　on your jacket
are finches
　　　　　I wanted to yell
　　　　　　　　　as you vanished
into a hotel
　　　　　to drink with
　　　　　　　　　your friends
there was nothing
　　　　　more
　　　　　　　　　you could do
after my attackers left
　　　　　before I got up
　　　　　　　　　I touched my face
almost tenderly

Postmortem

How did you meet

He stepped on my face, he stepped on my teeth

Was it love or lust

Can a hummingbird see that much

What happened when he touched you

The world spilled out

Do you recall his eyes

A cup & a bowl

& his voice

Possibly a mouse drank it

How did he make you feel

I am a fruitless tree, you are a fruitless tree

How did you cope

By nibbling away

How do you remember him

I make a smudge

1707 San Joaquin Avenue

*Federal authorities say sixty-nine suspected ~~illegal~~ immigrants,
including two children & an infant, have been rescued from a
drop house in Phoenix.*

—Associated Press

Wall clock covered with duct tape.
No tables. No couch. No doors—
even the bathroom door is missing.

Toilet cracked, clogged.
In the bathtub, cat litter.

Who smuggled you into the country? *Un mexicano.*
Who brought you to the house? *Un mexicano.*
Who took away your purse & cellphone? *Un mexicano.*

I don't smuggle. I coax—I'm brought to the casa

on the second day. By then, the whole damn place

reeks of armpits & mierda. I work with a perfumed scarf

tied around my cintura. Don't call me Juanga—

if I catch a pendejo insulting me, I snip off the tip

of his pinche tongue. Listen: I only touch the men.

The polleros, at my command, kick one into the baño,

force him to kneel in the bathtub, to call relatives.

Most quickly agree to pay the ransom. If they haggle,

I drag a blade across his rippling face. Slowly. Sweetly.

The polleros record it all. It's easier to hurt centro-

americanos. Those indios snatching pinche trabajos

that belong to our pinche gente. You should see

their eyes when I pull out the icepick. ¡A la verga!

ϕ

In the kitchen, stacks of buckets:

Clean Paws	Ever Clean Extra Strength
Arm & Hammer Scoopable	Pretty Cat Litter
Fresh Step Clay Litter	Fresh Step Extreme Odor Control

ф

How did you make it through those days?
When you hurt, you're not completely in the world.

His mother listens on the phone
as they order him to bend over.
When he refuses, they burn his back
with cigarettes, a blowtorch.
Then they force his legs apart.
His mother listens on the phone.

scar **Vanessa** Higinio Mireya Alexei Lun

ayeli

Pablo Martha **Lucas Ernesto Lupe**

Rodrigo Franciso **Juan Carmen**

Joel Roberto Mercedes Paty **Diego**

amona **Sandra** Martín **Daisy**

Alberto Lorna Luis

Saul Manuel Marco Jenni Blanca **Pau**

Isabel Ana Rocío Marcelo

nmanuel **Pedro Norma Esteban**

Julián Marcelo **Javier Natalie Erika**

Ruben **Antonio Carmen** Rafael Stefan

orna

Marín **Sara** Míro J**ordi Andrés**

César **Thalia Iván** Victor Fernando

Alex **Junior** Vickie Cassandra Nic

omán

Elias Gustavo Kostas Leo Mateo

Fábio Rachel Freddy Bianca

lomena Melissa **Enrique Yareli**

To Juan Doe #234

I only recognized your hair: short,
neatly combed. Our mother

would've been proud.
                    In the Sonoran Desert
your body became a slaughter-

house where faith & want were stunned,
hung upside down, gutted. We

                    were taught

to bring roses, to aim for the bush. Remember?
You tried to pork

a girl's armpit. In Border Patrol
                    jargon, the word

for border crossers is the same whether
                    they're alive or dead.
When I read his flesh fell

off the bones, my stomach rumbled,
                    my mouth

watered. Yesterday, our mother said,
                    "My high heels are killing me.
Let's go back to the funeral."

                    You were always

her favorite. Slow cooking a roast
melts the tough tissue between the muscle fibers;
tender meat remains.

Remember the time
I caught you pissing
                on a dog? You turned

away from me. In the small of your back
I thought I saw a face.
                        Split lip,
broken nose. It was a mask.
                I yanked it from your flesh.
        I wear it often.

Notes

The epigraph from Myriam Moscona is pulled from *Negro marfil / Ivory Black*, a book-length sequence translated by Jen Hofer (Les Figues Press, 2011).

An annotated draft of "Ceremonial" appeared on the cover of the *New York Times Book Review* in 2017. Thank you, Carl Marcum, for the title.

Testaments Scratched into a Water Station Barrel

The sequence has its roots in PINTURA : PALABRA, an ekphrasis project spearheaded by Francisco Aragón of Letras Latinas, the literary program of the University of Notre Dame's Institute for Latino Studies. Writers were asked to select a piece of art then write about it. I picked *Humane Borders Water Station* by Delilah Montoya, a haunting photograph of blue water station barrels in southern Arizona. (Humane Borders, a human rights organization, sets up & maintains water stations in the Arizona desert. The water stations are life-saving sources of water.)

After writing my ekphrastic poem, the water station barrels stayed with me—I kept imaging stories, rants, wishes & confessions that might be scratched into the blue of the barrels. Speakers began to arrive: Mexican & Central American immigrants making visible the worlds inside them. (Some of the language, though, belongs to racists who've vandalized water barrels.)

Then it dawned on me: the speakers were scratching time & again one water station barrel. So, in my mind, this one water station barrel morphed into a three-dimensional communal space, a lyrical expanse scored with human utterance.

The ending of [Apá, dying is boring. To pass las horas] riffs on the ending of "Dusting" by Rita Dove, which appears in *Thomas and Beulah* (Carnegie Mellon University Press, 1986).

The Portuguese in [Bought my luck] is pulled from "Holy Saturday" by Ana Cristina César, which appears in *At Your Feet,* a poetic sequence translated by Brenda Hillman & Helen Hillman, with Sebastião Edson Macedo, edited by Katrina Dodson (Parlor Press, 2018).

The ending of [Perro que no anda] was inspired by ants swarming a crucifix in *A Fire in My Belly*, a short film by David Wojnarowicz.

Juan Gabriel song titles are scattered throughout [Sombras]. Señora de las Sombras is another name for Nuestra Señora de la Santa Muerte.

[God is circling like a vulture] borrows song titles by Los Tigres del Norte.

The epigraph from Luis Muñoz is pulled from "Envío al Presente," a poem which appears in his book *Vecindad* (Visor Libros, 2018).

The language "kimono of pressed-together dust" in "Sentence" is pulled from "Song of the Restless Wind," by Don McKay, which appears in *Camber: Selected Poems* (McClelland & Stewart, 2014).

"Saguaro" is dedicated to Ofelia Zepeda.

"Autobiography of My Hungers" takes its title from a memoir by Rigoberto González.

"Song of the Open Road" takes its title from a poem by Walt Whitman. The epigraph is informed by "Newly Released FOIA Documents Shed Light on Border Patrol's Seemingly Limitless Authority," an article by Max Rivlin-Nadler, published online by the *Intercept* in 2019.

"Black Water" is dedicated to the memory of Agha Shahid Ali.

The title of "Around Every Circle Another Can Be Drawn" is taken from "Circles," an essay by Ralph Waldo Emerson. The ending of the poem reworks a quote by Saint Augustine of Hippo, which is quoted by Emerson in the same essay.

The answers in "Postmortem" are an assortment of Nahuatl proverbs & metaphors pulled from *Nahuatl Proverbs, Conundrums, and Metaphors*, collected by Bernardino de Sahagún & translated by Thelma D. Sullivan (Estudios de Cultura Nahuatl, 1963).

Some of the details in the sequence "1707 San Joaquin Avenue" were pulled from various newspaper articles on drop houses in Arizona.

Acknowledgments

The attentiveness & kindness of the following people nourished me as I wrote these poems:

Jim Johnstone, Alexandra Lytton Regalado, Declan Ryan, Don Share, Edvards Kuks, Steven Alvarez, Ocean Vuong, Peter Bienkowski, Michael Prior, Jenn Givhan, Keegan Lester, Eliza Rodriguez y Gibson, Rigoberto González, Patrick Cotter, Andrea Blancas Beltran, Rachel Morgan, Tyree Daye, Uk Lushi, David Tomas Martinez, Kyle Churney, Carl Phillips, Kevin A. González, Adam Clay, Tracy K. Smith, Kaveh Akbar, Matt Rader, Christopher Soto, Natalie Diaz, David Welch, Gary Dop, Sara P. Alvarez, Spencer Reece, Jenny Xie, Marcelo Hernandez Castillo, Heather Hughes, Erika L. Sánchez, Matt Wimberley, Francisco Aragón, Justin Evans & Manuel Muñoz.

My profound gratitude to the following institutions for providing time & space to work on these poems:

The Banff Centre, the MacDowell Colony, the National Endowment for the Arts & the Whiting Foundation.

I'd especially like to thank the Lewis Center for the Arts at Princeton University for a Hodder Fellowship, which allowed me to move back to Arizona to take care of my father as he recovered from a serious illness. During those scary months, in the quiet hours, I drafted many of the poems in the "Testaments" sequence.

I count myself lucky to work at North Carolina State University. Many thanks to my colleagues in the MFA program: Belle Boggs, John Kessel & Wilton Barnhardt.

A tip of the hat to the faculty & students of the Postgraduate Writers' Conference at Vermont College of Fine Arts & the low-residency MFA program at Pacific University for welcoming me.

Endless gratitude to Dorianne Laux & Joe Millar for making my life in Raleigh possible.

Felipe Baeza, what an honor to have your art on the cover of this book. Gracias.

To Jeff Shotts: thank you for your support, your patience & your editorial insight.

My gratitude to everyone at Graywolf Press. It's an honor to be part of the pack.

I don't have the language to articulate my love for my parents, Higinio & Socorro.

To my nieces & nephews: stop asking for money. Just joking. The check is in the mail.

Much love to my siblings: Mireya, Higinio, Martha & Martin.

A thousand thanks to the editors of the following journals & anthologies for publishing / reprinting the following poems.

Ambit (UK): "Black Water"
The New Republic: "Border Patrol Agent"
Poem-A-Day Series, Academy of American Poets: "Ceremonial"
Poetry: "Sentence," "Autobiography of My Hungers," "Córdoba," "Lines Written at Federico García Lorca Park," "To a Straight Man," "Postmortem," "To Juan Doe #234" & from the "Testaments Scratched into a Water Station Barrel" sequence: "[Apá, dying is boring. To pass las horas]," "[Bought my luck]," "[In a room with a terracotta door-knob   I slept]," "[In the desert, the moon]," [Perro que no anda]," "[Sombras]," "[Sometimes a wolf leaps out of a lion   last winter]," "[Before fleeing Toluca   I left a glass of water]," "[Far from highways I flicker]," "[God is circling like a vulture]"
Poetry London (UK): "Around Every Circle Another Can Be Drawn"
Wild Court (UK): "Guillotine"

"Ceremonial," "Sentence" & "Guillotine" were reprinted in *Reading Queer: Poetry in a Time of Chaos*, edited by Neil de la Flor & Maureen Seaton (Anhinga Press, 2018).

"To Juan Doe #234" was reprinted in *Poetry: A Writers' Guide and Anthology*, edited by Amorak Huey & W. Todd Kaneko (Bloomsbury Academic, 2018).

"Ceremonial" was reprinted in *Bettering American Poetry 2015*, edited by Amy King, Vanessa Angélica Villarreal, Nikki Wallschlaeger, Sarah Clark, Airea D. Matthews, Kenzie Allen, Eunsong Kim, Jason Koo, David Tomas Martinez & Hector Ramirez (Bettering Books, 2017).

"Border Patrol Agent" was reprinted in *Resistance, Rebellion, Life: 50 Poems Now*, edited by Amit Majmudar (Knopf, 2017).

"To a Straight Man" was reprinted in *Nepantla: An Anthology Dedicated to Queer Poets of Color*, edited by Christopher Soto (Nightboat Books, 2018).

"Song of the Open Road" appeared in *No Tender Fences: An Anthology of Immigrant & First-Generation American Poetry*, edited by Marina Carreira, Carla Sofia Ferreira & Kim Sousa.

EDUARDO C. CORRAL is the son of Mexican immigrants. His first book, *Slow Lightning*, won the Yale Younger Poets Prize. He is the recipient of a Whiting Award, a National Endowment for the Arts Fellowship & a Hodder Fellowship from Princeton University. He teaches in the MFA program in Creative Writing at North Carolina State University.

The text of *Guillotine* is set in Minion Pro. Book design by Ann Sudmeier. Composition by Bookmobile Design & Digital Publisher Services, Minneapolis, Minnesota. Manufactured by Versa Press on acid-free, 30 percent postconsumer wastepaper.